LIVING HISTORY

THE ANCIENT BRITONS

Stewart Ross

Illustrated by Mark Bergin

Living History

The American West
Ancient China
The Aztecs
Cavaliers and
  Roundheads
The Crusades
The Egyptians
Great Explorers
The Greeks
The Incas

The Middle Ages
The Normans
North American
  Indians
The Romans
The Saxons
The Stuarts
The Tudors
The Victorians
The Vikings

477729

Editor: Nick Wallwork

First published in 1987 by
Wayland (Publishers) Ltd
61 Western Road, Hove,
East Sussex BN3 1JD, England

© Copyright 1987
Wayland (Publishers) Ltd

Phototypeset by
Kalligraphics Ltd, Redhill, Surrey
Printed and bound in Belgium by
Casterman S.A.

British Library Cataloguing in
Publication Data
Ross, Stewart
  The Ancient Britons. – (Living history)
  1. Man, Prehistoric – Great Britain –
  Juvenile literature   2. Great Britain –
  Social life and customs – To 1066 –
  Juvenile literature
  I. Title   II. Series
  936.1   GN805

  ISBN 1–85210–001–X

All the words in the text which
appear in **bold** are explained in
the glossary on page 28.

Contents

Who were the Ancient Britons?

The Ancient Britons were the first people who lived in the British Isles. They were groups of hunters who sailed to Britain thousands of years ago. They were followed many years later by groups of farmers. This time is known as the Stone Age because people used stone tools.

The last Ancient Britons to arrive were the Celts. They came in **tribes**, such as the Iceni. You can see them landing in the picture opposite. The Celts were the first Britons who knew how to make iron tools. The men in the picture above are building a fence around their village to keep out wild animals. There were wolves and bears in Britain then.

The village

The Ancient Britons lived in small villages. Many of these were built on hills, where they could easily be defended from attackers. Some villages, like the one below, were built on **stilts** in the middle of a lake. This made it very difficult for an enemy to attack the village.

Most people in the village were farmers or
servants. Some men were **craftsmen,**
others were soldiers. The priest, in the
picture above, was called a druid. Each
tribe had a king or queen who was
advised by nobles.

At home

Ancient Britons lived in very simple houses made of wood or stone. The roofs were **thatched.** There was only one room in which everyone ate, slept and worked. Sometimes in the winter they shared their houses with their cattle. The women in the house below are **weaving** cloth to make into clothes. The picture opposite shows how they stored grain in pits.

There were no schools at that time.
Children helped in the home or in the
fields and learned all they needed to know
from their parents. The language they
spoke was different from ours, but very
few Ancient Britons could read or write.

Food and drink

The Ancient Britons ate a great deal of bread. They had to harvest the corn by hand, cutting it with **sickles**. You can see two men doing this below. The corn was then ground using stones and baked into bread in clay ovens.

Britons also ate plenty of meat. This came from farm animals, or wild animals such as deer or **boar**, which they caught by hunting. They ate using only their fingers and knives. The picture above shows a great feast. The Ancient Britons liked to drink huge amounts of beer at feasts. They sat on the floor, told stories, sang songs and soon became very noisy.

15

Clothes

As you can see in the small picture below, the clothes of the Ancient Britons were not very different from our own. The women wore long brightly coloured dresses. The men wore trousers and **tunics.** Most clothes were made of wool or leather.

The Ancient Britons liked to look their best. Most men wore moustaches, while men and women took great care of their hair. They washed it often and arranged it with plaits or pins. However, they could look very frightening going into battle. They painted their bodies with **woad**, like the warriors in the picture below.

British crafts

The men below are **blacksmiths**. Blacksmiths were among the most important men in the village. They made tools and weapons by heating up iron strips and beating them into shape. Before about 500 BC the Ancient Britons did not know how to make iron. Instead they used **bronze**, a much softer metal.

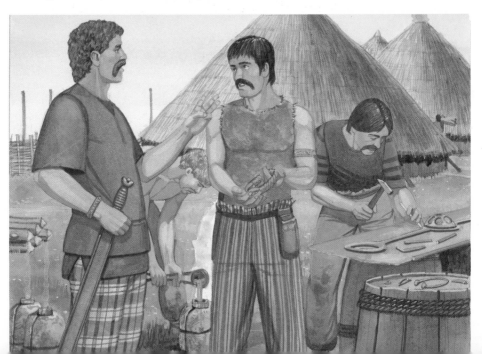

The beautiful necklace in the picture above is made of gold. Ancient British craftsmen made lovely jewellery which was worn by the rich families of the village. The warriors decorated their swords and shields with bronze and gold designs, and wore heavy bronze jewellery.

19

Strange gods

The Ancient Britons believed in many gods. Each tribe had its own god who led them into battle.

They also thought that there were spirits
in trees, streams and animals. The man in
the picture opposite has thrown a gold
ring into a lake to please the god who lives
there. The Celts of the Iron Age believed
that people went to the Otherworld when
they died. The dead nobleman in the
picture above is being prepared for his
journey to the Otherworld. In his grave he
has all the things that he will need for his
new life.

War

The Ancient British tribes spent much of their time fighting each other. Some tribes lived in hillforts, like the one in the picture below. Hillforts were surrounded by wooden walls, ditches and earth banks.

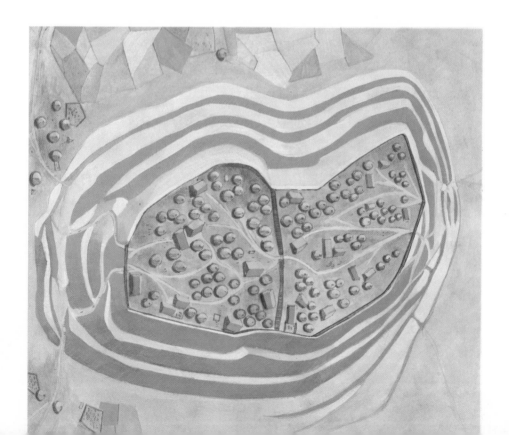

The Ancient Britons fought with spears, swords and shields. When fighting in the open they used fast **chariots** pulled by horses. Sometimes these had large knives or spikes on their wheels.

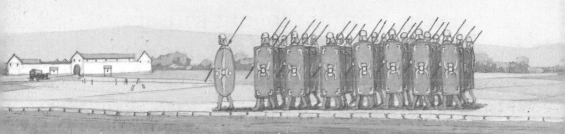

The arrival of the Romans

About 2,000 years ago the British Isles were invaded by a new group of people. They were called the Romans. The powerful Roman army had already conquered the rest of Europe and now wanted to make Britain part of its **empire.** After many battles the Ancient Britons were defeated.

24

When the Romans arrived all the ways of
the Ancient Britons were destroyed. The
Romans brought a new language, new
clothes and new gods. They built fine
buildings and roads. Many of the Ancient
Britons, as you can see in this picture,
were led off to be slaves or were made to
work for the Romans.

Things to do

Woad

The blue paint with which Ancient British warriors decorated themselves was called woad. You could paint yourself with face paints or poster paints to look like an Ancient Briton. Don't use felt tip pens because the colour doesn't wash off easily.

Stonehenge

The Ancient Britons of the Bronze Age built the famous monument called Stonehenge. You can make a model of Stonehenge out of painted matchboxes on a green card base. You can make Stonehenge as it is today, or you can make it as it was in the time of the Ancient Britons, with all the stones standing in place.

27

Glossary

Blacksmiths   People who are very clever at making things out of iron.

Boar   A wild pig with tusks.

Bronze   A metal made by mixing copper and tin.

Chariots   Light two-wheeled carts pulled by horses, usually only used in battle.

Craftsmen   Men skilled at working with their hands.

Empire   A large area of land that has been conquered by one country.

Sickles   Curved knives used for cutting grass or corn.

Stilts   Long wooden poles used by the Ancient Britons to lift their houses clear of a lake.

Thatched   Roofed with straw or reeds.

Tribes   Large groups of similar people living together.

Tunics   Coats that have no opening at the front.

Weaving   A way of putting threads together to make cloth.

Woad   Blue body paint. The paint was made from flowers grown especially for this purpose.

Books to read

Discovering the Ancient Past by Michael Gibson
 (Macdonald, 1976)
Growing up in Ancient Britain by Amanda Clark
 (Batsford, 1981)
Invaded Island by R.J. Unstead (Macdonald, 1971)
Living in Prehistoric Times by Jane Chisholm
 (Usborne, 1982)
Stone Age to Iron Age by Jane R. Osborn
 (Longman, 1968)

Picture acknowledgements
Some of the illustrations in this book were originally used in *Boudicca and the Ancient Britons* in Wayland's Life and Times series.

Index